SNOW PATROL
UP TO NOW

WISE PUBLICATIONS
part of The Music Sales Group

London / New York / Paris / Sydney / Copenhagen / Berlin / Madrid / Tokyo

PUBLISHED BY
WISE PUBLICATIONS
14-15 BERNERS STREET, LONDON W1T 3LJ, UK.

EXCLUSIVE DISTRIBUTORS:
MUSIC SALES LIMITED
DISTRIBUTION CENTRE,
NEWMARKET ROAD, BURY ST EDMUNDS, SUFFOLK, IP33 3YB, UK.
MUSIC SALES PTY LIMITED
20 RESOLUTION DRIVE, CARINGBAH, NSW 2229, AUSTRALIA.

ORDER NO. AM999636
ISBN 978-1-84938-413-1

EDITED BY JENNI WHEELER.
MUSIC ARRANGED BY VASCO HEXEL.
MUSIC ENGRAVED BY PAUL EWERS MUSIC DESIGN.

PRINTED IN THE EU.

WWW.MUSICSALES.COM

CHASING CARS

Words & Music by Gary Lightbody, Nathan Connolly,
Jonathan Quinn, Paul Wilson & Tom Simpson

6

Forget what we're told
before we get
too old.
Show me a garden that's
bursting into life.

here,   if I just lay here,___   would you lie

with me___ and___ just for - get the world?___   For-get what we're

told___   be-fore we get too old.___   Show me a

gar - den___ that's___ burst-ing in-to life.___   All that I

CHOCOLATE

**Words & Music by Gary Lightbody, Jonathan Quinn,
Nathan Connolly & Mark McLelland**

15

CRACK THE SHUTTERS

Words & Music by Paul Wilson, Gary Lightbody,
Jonathan Quinn, Nathan Connolly & Tom Simpson

1.You cool your bed-warm hands_____ down_____ on the bro-

2. It's been min-utes, it's been days, it's been

-ken_____ ra-di-a-tor._____

all I_____ will re-mem-ber._____

THE GOLDEN FLOOR

Words & Music by Paul Wilson, Gary Lightbody,
Jonathan Quinn, Nathan Connolly & Tom Simpson

1. Tell me that you want to dance. __ I want to feel your pulse on

(4.) fold - ed in the bread you made. __ You're cold un - til my bod - y

Just treat me like a sto-len glance to your-self.
bathes you in the heat I kept a-side all these days.

To Coda ⊕

2. A dark shape on a gold - en floor, a sleep-ing
(3.) peas - ant in your prin - cess arms,

plan-et with a molt - en core. From a - bove we'd cut a slow eight
pen - ni - less with on - ly charm. As we're lev-elled by the low, hot

1.
shape and much more.
lights and dis - armed.

3. I'm a

2.

HANDS OPEN

Words & Music by Paul Wilson, Gary Lightbody,
Jonathan Quinn, Nathan Connolly & Tom Simpson

JUST SAY YES

Words & Music by Gary Lightbody & Garret Lee

31

ON/OFF

Words & Music by Gary Lightbody,
Jonathan Quinn & Mark McClelland

OPEN YOUR EYES

Words & Music by Paul Wilson, Gary Lightbody,
Jonathan Quinn, Nathan Connolly & Tom Simpson

RUN

Words & Music by Gary Lightbody, Jonathan Quinn,
Mark McClelland, Nathan Connolly & Iain Archer

Light up, light up, as if you___ have___ a choice.

E - ven if you can - not___ hear___ my voice, I'll be right be - side you___ dear.___

THE PLANETS BEND BETWEEN US

Words & Music by Paul Wilson, Gary Lightbody,
Jonathan Quinn, Nathan Connolly & Tom Simpson

1. The win-ter's marked the earth. It's floored
(2.) -ing speech bub-bles seem to hold

SET THE FIRE TO THE THIRD BAR

Words & Music by Paul Wilson, Gary Lightbody,
Jonathan Quinn, Nathan Connolly & Tom Simpson

SIGNAL FIRE

Words & Music by Paul Wilson, Gary Lightbody,
Jonathan Quinn, Nathan Connolly & Tom Simpson

scream - ing__ out,__ but the sound was trapped__ deep__ in me.__

2. All I__ want - ed just sped right__ past__ me__ while I was
3. In the__ con - fusion and the af - ter - math_____ you

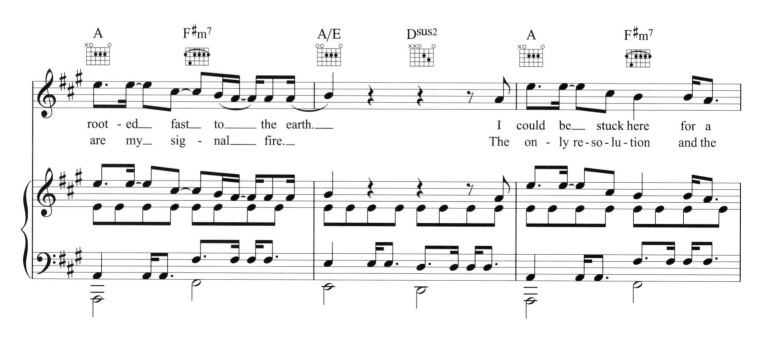

root - ed__ fast__ to_____ the earth.__ I could be__ stuck here for a
are my__ sig - nal__ fire.__ The on - ly re - so - lu - tion and the

All__ this fear__ falls__ a-way to leave me__ na - ked.

Hold__ me close,__ 'cause I need you to guide me__ to safe - ty.

1.

No, I don't want to

wait for - ev - er. No, I don't want to wait for - ev - er.

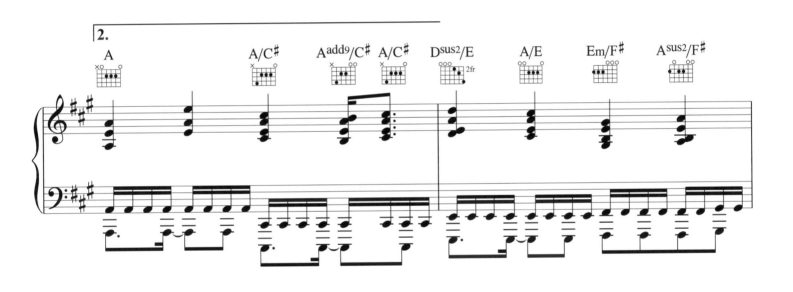

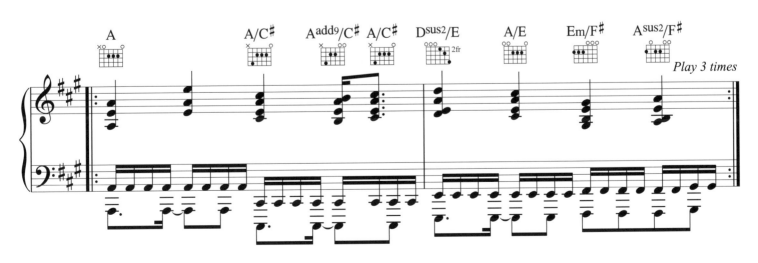

Play 3 times

There_ you are_____ stand - ing right in front of____ me.____

There_ you are_____ stand - ing right in front of____ me.____

All____ this fear_____ falls_ a-way to leave me____ na - ked,.

SPITTING GAMES

Words & Music by Gary Lightbody, Jonathan Quinn,
Mark McClelland & Nathan Connolly

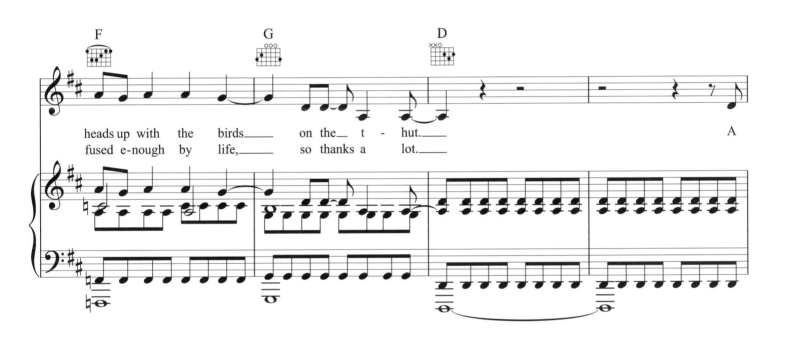

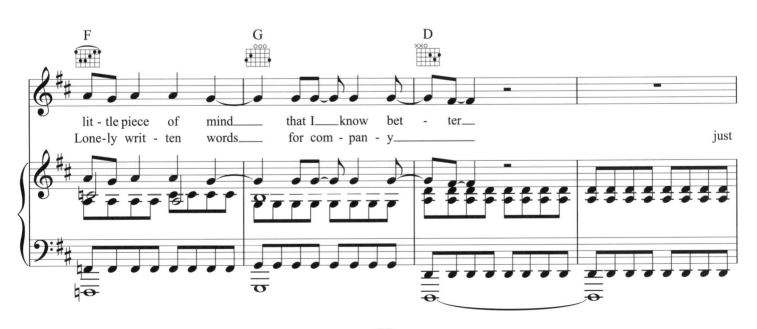

than the plain dis - grace_____ of all__ my let - ters..

raise the roof this once_____ and fol - low me._____

Ooh,____ ooh,____ ooh,____ ooh.____

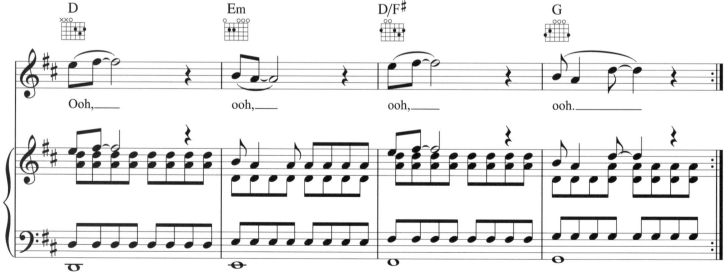

Ooh,____ ooh,____ ooh,____ ooh.____

TAKE BACK THE CITY

Words & Music by Paul Wilson, Gary Lightbody,
Jonathan Quinn, Nathan Connolly & Tom Simpson

1. Take back the cit-y for your-self to-night.
2. All these years la-ter and it's kill-ing me.
3. Tell me you nev-er want-ed more than this

I'll take back the cit-y for me.
Your bro-ken re-cords in words.
and I will stop talk-ing now.

YOU'RE ALL I HAVE

Words & Music by Paul Wilson, Gary Lightbody,
Jonathan Quinn, Nathan Connolly & Tom Simpson

1. Strain this cha - os, turn it in - to light.____
2. You're ci - ne - ma - tic ra - zor sharp,____

85

123456789